THE RAINBOW IN YOUR HANDS

Books by
Albert Roy Davis

Anatomy of Biomagnetics

Magnet and Magnetic Fields or
Healing by Magnets

Books by
Albert Roy Davis and
Walter C. Rawls, Jr.

The Magnetic Blueprint of Life

The Rainbow in Your Hands

The Magnetic Effect

Magnetism and Its Effects on the Living System

The Rainbow in Your Hands

Albert Roy Davis
and
Walter C. Rawls, Jr.

Acres U.S.A. Kansas City, Missouri

Acknowledgement
To
The Artist of Our Front Cover

Mr. Seth W. Thomas
Studio One
Green Cove Springs, Florida 32043

First Printing, April 1976
Second Printing, June 1977
Third Printing, January 1979
Fourth Printing, May 1980
Fifth Printing, November 1981
Sixth Printing, April 1984
Seventh Printing, July 1988
Eighth Printing, July 1992

ISBN: 0-911311-16-5
Library of Congress catalog card number: 92-72636
Printed in the United States of America

Contents

Introduction

The title of our book, *The Rainbow in Your Hands,* expresses that Natural and God-Given Energy all men, women and children possess regardless of race, faith or creed.

You hold this greatness in your hands. By your very thoughts you can offer help, good will, happiness to all around you. You can live a better life. All you have to do is have an understanding about your natural energy and direct your hands toward building a more natural world.

We will explain the presence and use of this energy. You will be the judge concerning its effectiveness.

The Rainbow in Your Hands is a very real energy. You can direct this energy to help yourself and all living things.

The great healers and comforters of history used this natural power. Under one term or another it is known in the philosophy and structure of every civilization of record on this earth. It has been called the life force, the divine spark, the essence of life, mana, prana, akasia, kundalini, li, ch'i, odic force, orgone energy, L-fields and many other names in many languages. Where it is not mentioned, its presence is self-evident by its power and effect.

A mother's gentle touch to the fevered brow of her child brings a relief no medicine could hope to afford. The smile of the child in return is the greatest reward the mother could have. They are both joined in a spiritual unity when the natural laying on of hands takes place.

In our previous books, *Magnetism and Its Effects on the Living System* and *The Magnetic Effect*, we have presented from many years of research a new scientific understanding of the natural energy of magnetism. In this book we give you results of our research which indicate that the energies of the hands contain, give, and transmit two forms of potential natural energies, each having an effect on the senses, feelings, and bioelectrical activity in and among mankind.

This is a science. Any of you can reproduce our findings. Science is also Knowledge, and we will share our research knowledge with you. Many of you will instinctively agree with our findings. You have used this power, whether knowing or unknowing, from your natural energy being.

We have studied and measured the energy in the hands of many persons. Our new understandings in our previous books show the reproducible effects in our animal research, and the relation of our discoveries to physics and other sciences. Our work as scientists affirms our belief that the energy in your hands is God's natural power. As matters will occur that are meant to occur, we trust in God in this presentation to you. May it strengthen confidence to you and those you aid in your efforts. In our troubled world this may be the time in history when each of you should understand and use this natural energy for the good of mankind.

If you read this book with calmness, allowing your inner senses to guide your thoughts, and if you will sincerely, with patience, apply the techniques we will explain, you will improve your own well-being. You will improve your relations with other peoples. You will know that you are using God's own natural energy to help others in their relations. Life will have more meaning to you. The world in which we live will improve in your view, and in the view of those you aid, with this natural energy that shows no prejudice. Proper use will give peace and contentment to your surroundings. You have this power and the techniques have been proved. The only prescription you need is your effort of calm resolve to apply the proper techniques with your own God-Given Natural Energy.

The Authors

THE RAINBOW IN YOUR HANDS

1
Nature and You

A rainbow has a visual display of beauty and expression in the splendor of its colorful presentation. It holds the spectrum of all energies known to man. It is God's gift to all mankind and to all the natural forms of animals, plants and flowers. While man is considered the highest of intelligence within the animal kingdom, he has much to learn from the animals, plants and all the natural surrounding life.

Man has never been an island to himself. It is inconceivable that he could ever be this way, not in his present state of being. Nature is always with man; Man is always with Nature. They are a part of one to the other as one together never apart. Man may try to lock out Nature; he may succeed to some degree but he will never succeed completely. It is impossible and cannot be accomplished. Thank God, that this is the way of Life.

Man's understanding of intelligence is not Nature's conception of this word. Nature is all-knowing as Nature and God are one. The more that man progresses in his understanding of Nature, the more man is intelligent. To have intelligence per se would be complete realization with Nature and with God. Man progresses or he does not progress, and in civilization he has not been successful. He has shut out Nature and thus he has shut out God. He has raised artificial idols of material objects and beliefs with his free will, that is God-granted, and used this gift to turn against Nature.

All mankind exists within a very narrow spectrum of the life forces found on Earth. Man has developed means of survival and existence he calls "civilization." We cannot accept that only man's structure of his present existence is civilization. We must consider that each life form has its own well-developed structure. We define the meaning to include all living systems, animals of all types, kinds, sizes, plants, flowers, microbes, bacteria, germs and other life forms.

Webster defines *civilization* as meaning "to raise up from barbarism, to introduce order and civic organization among the masses of that life order." Civilization occurred among the plants and lower animals long before man became aware of order and civil behavior. Man is far from civilized today in behavior to his fellow man. And it is not civilization for political leaders to enforce their order of life. Nor is civilization anarchy. Nature has provided a universal law of all Life, and Peace and Order is the rule. This is the nature of man and this is the nature of all species. This is the ultimate in your progression, Peace and Order with Nature. Any man, species, political or social structure, that strives against this progression is artificial and unnatural. What is man to profit if he gain the whole world but suffer the loss of his soul? Man, not content with natural ways, strives to improve upon Nature instead of working with

Nature. Thus man seeks to destroy the very basis on which all natural life and order is established.

We have been instrumental in aiding the education of thousands of young persons. Science courses from our laboratory have been translated and adopted in many foreign countries for grade and high school levels of learning. The young people we came to know all expressed their willingness to learn the mysteries of Nature. They wanted to believe, and when shown the truths of Nature's works they did believe. Persons of all ages want to believe—in themselves, in Nature and in God. You want to believe, and you do believe, if you listen to your inner voice, your inner conscience, with calm sincerity.

Nature is responsible for the laws by which all life is born, lives and dies on this earth. We know that the elements that make up our physical existence and that of plants, bacteria and other life forms, are transformed after what we call physical death into elements of matter that provide a continuous cycle of existence without end. Scientists can prove much of this transference in the laboratory. The great laboratory proof we lack is the continuity of intelligence, personality, the Soul. A number of outstanding scientists now believe this laboratory proof is not far from being discovered.

Have you ever considered where the idea of God started? Of course, you will say, it started with God himself. But consider, if God did not exist, and Life was not total in its continuity, why has the belief in God persisted? The Nature of a being cannot be destroyed. It can be hidden and it can be ignored, but through all history to our knowledge, the Nature of God has persisted, for discovery and progression in man and his societies.

If God wishes in his divine plan for laboratory proof of his existence then through his will it will be shown. Would you believe what your eyes would then see, what could be reproduced over and over again? You would no more believe in this manner than you fail to believe your inner Nature telling you that continuity of Life and God are truth.

The lower animals have an instinctive intelligence to their environment that is lacking in man. They know how to use the elements in their environment to provide them with health and relieve their illness and discomfort. Nature gives them the knowledge to survive with Nature, while man seems to have lost his security in a natural environment.

Nature has provided the Laws by which all matter, immaterial and material, airs, gases, living and animate life function. These Laws contain unwritten orders that control all systems of life and behavior, including health and sickness. Each and every type of illness has natural laws of progression or arrest procedures.

Only lack of belief in understanding his natural ability prevents man from arresting his complaints and those of others. It is man's destiny that he must strive in his progression to uncover the well-hidden secrets of Nature. From the behavior of the simple atom to the most complex molecules of man, laws of behavior are at work, reaching through space, to the sun, moon, planets, stars, trillions of light-years into the vastness of space. For a law to be a natural law it must operate within its procedure on a distant star as on this planet. Without natural laws there would be no foresight in a system of progressive behavior.

If the progressive behavior of Life is under natural law from birth to physical death, endless in reproductivity, then all things are prearranged to occur in the order Nature intended. This does not eliminate alternate paths of travel and behavior in this cycle. Nor does it deny the practice of a spiritual life as more comfortable and secure, and more intelligent. Once you progress your intelligence with God, you will not forget your experience, and you will want that experience again. It is so simply up to you if the experience reoccurs. You cannot limit Nature. You cannot limit God. You cannot limit the conscience of humanity.

Now, you say, what is this? We're talking about Nature and God, and civilization, and so on. Why go into all this? The answer to that question is that you will be better able to use your natural energies for yourself and others if you have an understanding of how you fit into Nature. You will then draw on Nature's energies with no great difficulty. The techniques we present will be as child's play to you.

One of our great problems in Life is that we live in a world of authority and direction imposed by other men, as well as ourselves. Whether by fear, ignorance, greed or other self-imposed restraints, we do not awake our inner courage to properly investigate nor accept existing knowledge of Nature and humanity.

Don't say you are not at fault because you are not

fooling anyone. We are all at fault. There are no perfect human beings in this existence. Realize this and look at your good side, listen to your inner voice; you're not such a bad person. Each in his own way is as good or better than another. But if you dwell on this kind of thinking, be careful, for you may lose your inner voice through your pride and self-righteousness. Try to keep a calm sincerity with yourself and with God. You will then be pleasantly surprised at your happenings and fulfillment in this life.

It is the study and knowledge of Nature, that through the grace of God is revealed, that progress is achieved. When this basic fundamental of human existence is overlooked, or in many instances narrowly construed, we selfishly limit our own progression, as we limit our understanding of Nature. A new thought, a new idea, a new concept and discovery, should leave us that more humble in the all-powerful presence of Nature's works. When we discover and explain a truth to our living, no matter how miraculous that truth may be to our comprehension, we tend to term the progress that of civilization rather than of Nature. There can be no progress in civilization without our progress in understanding Nature. The more you learn of Nature the more you realize that man more often breaks the Laws of Nature governing his health and welfare by his behavior than do the lower animals.

One of the Laws of Nature has to do with electricity. Ohm's Law allows electrical current and voltage to be computed mathematically. A known amount of current and voltage will produce a known amount of power.

This law existed long before man knew of electricity. Man did not make the behavior laws of electricity.

Electricity and Magnetism always exist together, as Nature and God are always together. Man is a bioelectrical animal and he is also a biomagnetic animal. Man is a walking, breathing generator of natural energies we call electromagnetic, as well as all forms of Life.

In the study of man and his electromagnetic Nature we have discovered techniques to aid your ability to give healing and relief to fellow human beings by the laying on of hands. You will also be giving healing and relief to yourself as you practice these techniques. Laying on of hands was practiced thousands of years ago. You will find it mentioned in great books and writings of many civilizations.

In the language that we use, what exactly is energy? Energy, regardless of kind and description, is motion. Biological electricity is motion of atoms, as man and all material or immaterial matters on earth is composed of atoms. The atom is a producer of both electricity and magnetism, and man is a bioelectromagnetic animal, or biomagnetic.

Man can use this energy he is manufacturing to aid other human beings and to communicate with other life forms. These are facts governed by their own Laws of behavior and reproducible results. Despite scientific theorists in disagreement, the facts speak for themselves.

For a scientist to accept a Law, it must be predicted, reproduced, time and time again, anywhere by any person qualified and equipped. This could be a method, system of behavior, mathematical, physical or immaterial, according to its Nature. This is not inventing. Man does not invent. He only discovers that which already exists, yet was unknown or unprovable to man. Scientists base the understanding of a Law on its ability to reproduce. Its very existence depends on this natural behavior. Interesting here to consider that scientists can be incorrect but Nature can never be. Did you know that most scientists do not believe in predestination? This is the belief that God has decreed all events unchangeable from beginning to eternity. But if scientists agree that Laws must be reproducible, how can they then state that predestination is not possible?

If Nature were not predictable then we would have no Laws, for the scientists or for anyone. A Law must be predictable, operating on a predetermined course. Thus we find an inconsistency in the scientist who will use primary laws and discoveries in an attempt to disprove the existence of God.

We have undertaken in this book to prove the existence of natural Laws that are reproducible, wherein you can use the energies in your hands to affect other human beings, living systems and non-living systems. If we can show you the techniques, and you can reproduce the effects, then we have established reasonable cause to believe that the laying on of hands has a scientific basis that deserves further serious investigations.

We also believe that our research has reached that point where this information should be available to those interested in advancing the science of Natural Healing, removed from the realm of old-fashioned superstitions to its proper place in the natural sciences, based on reproducible effects we will disclose.

Let us summarize what we have presented in this first chapter that can help you in applying the techniques we will explain.

1. Man and Nature are always together, and they cannot be separated.
2. The more man progresses in his understanding of Nature, the more man is intelligence.
3. Nature and God are one.
4. Nature, as God, has Laws of behavior, and Peace and Order is the rule. The ultimate in your progression is Peace and Order with Nature.
5. You believe in Nature and in God if you will listen to your inner voice with calm sincerity.
6. All Life is a continuous cycle of existence without end. Thus, a Natural Law is endless in reproductivity and is predetermined.
7. Knowledge of Nature, which is intelligence, is revealed through the grace of God.
8. A Law of Nature is that man, and all living things, are electromagnetic. Man is a walking, breathing generator of natural energies.
9. All energy is motion, in man and in all material and immaterial matter.
10. You can use your natural energies to practice the laying on of hands effectively, if you know the proper techniques, and this is Science.

2
Proving the Unprovable

The difference between superstition and reproducible facts rests entirely in one's ability to reproduce a happening, whatever its Nature may be. Therefore, if the hands of man, as the paws of lower animals, offer some form of relief to suffering, then the energy the hands possess has to exist. If it exists, then what is it? It is Nature, but how can we explain this particular existence for reproducible Laws? Any procedure that is used time and time again must have very little if any variables.

Your authors have an extensive background in researching the effects of magnetism on the living system. Three books have recently been published, *Magnetism and Its Effects on the Living System* and *The Magnetic Effect* (Exposition Press, Hicksville, New York) and *The Anatomy of Biomagnetics,* available only from our laboratory. These books were the product of more than twenty years of research on how a magnet's two poles offer different potential energies that will affect living systems with reproducible effects when properly applied. This applies to seeds, bacteria, germ culture, enzymes, proteins and, in brief, all living systems.

The unseen energies of magnetism affect water, fluids, solids, masses, airs and gases. Therefore, if these energies affect all atoms of matter, and each atom in itself functions as a magnet, you can understand the importance of harnessing these energies to perform reproducible happenings that are predictable with computer exactness.

Facts Are Reproducible

Our research findings are not theory, as a theory is what someone believes happens, or may happen. We base our research on provable, reproducible facts. Before we published our work in a paper or a book, months, usually years, of practical laboratory research are our back-up to our presentation. These are our credentials in identifying the energies in the hands and paws of living creatures.

Energies Are Transmittable

These energies are transmittable. They can leave a point and arrive at another point. Do the hands of man have the ability of containing an energy that can be transmitted to another entity, person or object from the fingers or palms? Research proves this can and does occur.

Forms of Energy

What form of energy is in the hands, the fingers, the palms, that can be transmitted? We have mentioned our research that proves an unseen energy is transmitted from each pole of a magnet. This work we used as our basis for investigating the energies in the hands.

In our earlier research there were no available instruments that could properly detect, record and measure the minute amounts of human biological voltages, currents and fields. We had to design our own instruments we believed would measure microscopic currents flowing around and through the hands, fingers, palms and fingertips.

Another difficulty we encountered was the strong pulses of the human or lower animal heartbeat that appeared on the surface of the skin over the entire body. This was an interference with our instrument pickup of the less obvious electromagnetic voltages and currents. We designed, then redesigned, our instruments with filter networks that removed the heartbeat interference, allowing only the measurement of actual skin voltages and currents. Going still further we came up with a microgalvometer with sensitivity to measure not only microvoltages but also the currents of these energies. And, of greater importance, their identification of positive or negative potential.

Positive and Negative Energies

We kept in mind that magnetism and electricity can exist only together, and we considered our basic work that the two poles of all magnets have two potential forms of energies. We realized that the north-seeking pole is the South pole, the south-seeking pole the North pole of all magnets. This discovery of the two dissimilar energies in a magnet has been proved, by hundreds of other scientists reproducing our work, to be correct, although the major part of the scientific community has yet to accept this Law. The South pole presents a Positive energy, whereas the North pole presents a Negative energy. Each energy has been supported by its separate use on thousands of biological living systems. Equally as many tests were run on water, fluids, solids, chemicals, proteins and enzymes, and the results were of computer exactness. The evidence was substantial that we were working with natural energies found in all living and non-living matter. Magnets could harness these energies. The energies harnessed could be used by man correctly or wrongly for desired results. Their presence was not restricted to harnessing by the use of magnets.

Was the natural energy in the hands similar to the two different energies we found exist in all magnets? The answer was forthcoming in dramatic affirmation. We thought this was the answer, but how could we set out to prove we were correct? As scientists we were looking for laboratory proof that could be reproduced time and time again with similar results.

Reproducible Effects of Energies

We set up experiments with biological systems using the North pole and South pole separately, with a control biological system without either applied energy. In a number of experiments, the biological systems were as exact as feasible, making allowance for known measured variables. We then looked for any change in the energy recordings of the biological systems by the use of a separate pole energy. The results were so remarkable that we had difficulty in believing what was taking place before our eyes. The South pole energy showed a measured increase in activity and strength in the biological system, whereas the systems with the North pole energy recorded a reduction in activity and strength. The South pole energy acted for a positive reaction, the North pole energy a negative reaction, to both living and non-living biological systems. The controls, as expected, registered no changes. Different shapes, types, compositions of magnets were tested and the results were similar. This was proof there was a difference between the energies coming from the separate poles of magnets.

Another dramatic effect occurred when we found that the North pole energy placed against a painful area would reduce the pain. Further results indicated that, where infections had caused pain, the infections were reduced, arrested, and in time controlled, to slowly disappear completely. This was with careful timed placement of the North pole magnetic energy against the infected and painful areas. Our book *The Magnetic Effect* describes exactly how these and hundreds of other research cases were affected by this work with biological systems.

It was of interest to record that the South pole energy would increase infection and pain. We determined the North pole energy as a reducing effect energy, the South pole as an increasing effect energy. The South pole energy increased life and added strength, which included encouraging infection, because bacteria and germs are living systems, as is man.

Remember for a moment what the requirements are in the modern scientific community. For a new discovery to be accepted as a scientific law it must be reproducible time and time again. Any person capable of performing, when advised of the procedure, can repeat the experiment every time with little or no variables. Our research alone has been on more than five thousand test cases. The results have been similar, with variations plus or minus within ten percent. These variations are mainly due to climate, very hot dry to very hot wet or cold weather. This was on purpose as we wanted normal environments for these experiments rather than a "glass cage" that we considered too controlled for natural effects.

Did the hands have energies that may act in a manner similar to the separate pole effect of a magnet? Yes, a similar reaction does take place, and we measured these effects with hundreds of experiments on living and non-living biological systems.

3

Generating Your Own Energy

You may be acquainted with some of the many books written on the possibility that the human body generates its own kind of animal magnetism. You may not know that even in the scientific laboratory this is now a fact, not a possibility.

In our next chapter we will explain how you can use the healing power in your hands. Here, in this chapter, we present more background for your understanding and proper use of this energy. The knowledge that you have of the energy in you will assist your effectiveness in its use for others and yourself, with The Rainbow in Your Hands.

Do All Persons Generate This Energy?

Yes, the human body, and all biological life, generates an unseen energy that is normally applied to defend against bacteria, viruses and infection. It is produced when needed, and it is directed to the area in need. This occurs in seconds' time or less after damage occurs to any area of the living system. Remarkable, but true, this natural biological energy is in every living system.

For our purposes, in considering the human system,

the instruments we designed measured the generation of this energy. For example, take a location of a broken leg bone. Knowing the average normal recorded voltage of that area, and measuring the location voltage after a break, there is a sharp rise in negative voltage at the point or area of the break. This striking rise in the negative voltage remains high above normal until all healing of the bone and area has occurred. After healing is accomplished the negative voltage returns to its normal average level. This is an important natural process.

Life Depends on Negative Energy

(1) Injury. (2) Negative Voltage Rises. (3) Healing Occurs. (4) Negative Voltage Returns to Normal.

These measurements were conducted on a number of willing human subjects and different species of animals with remarkable similarity of recordings regardless of species. The amount of negative energy your system can generate will determine if you will overcome an infection, injury or physical death.

This discovery was used in our development of applying magnetic energy externally to the bone without surgery to heal bone regrowth, and these findings have been published. The general accepted practice of using energy involves implanting pins into the two segments of a broken bone by surgery. The pins are connected by small insulated wires to a flashlight battery with controls to limit the flow of negative and positive electricity across the fracture.

If our discovery of the external separate negative energy for aiding healing and bone growth was adopted, which other scientists and medical researchers can easily reproduce by following our published instructions, this would go a long way in eliminating unnecessary hospitalization, medical bills and surgery in this matter.

Energies of Magnet and Biological System Similar

Considering from our research that the energy in a magnet is similar to the negative and positive energy in the biological system, the more understanding you have concerning these magnetic energies the better you will understand how they generate within your own system.

The North pole of a magnet delivers a very powerful Negative energy much higher than the normal body magnetic negative energy. Thus, it stands to reason, and has been proved, that applying the North pole energy of a magnet to an area in distress, such as a broken bone, infected or swollen area, there would be an additional increase to the body's own natural energy that is trying to overcome the problem.

And applying the South pole Positive energy externally to the main part of the broken bone, and the North pole Negative energy on the side away from the main bone, acts to encourage the healing better in this instance than the use of only one natural energy.

What is occurring with surgery, implanted pins, wires and flashlight battery, is moving current from the positive electrical post to the negative electrical post. In your own body your energy flows in a similar manner. We reproduced this procedure in our experiments to see what was actually happening in the human system. The main bone slowly dissolved some of its bone calcium and was drawn to the detached bone end, the current flowing from positive to negative making this possible. Also, some of the calcium from the surrounding body fluids was drawn to and across the broken area.

We then reproduced the entire project in a glass test jar. We took a well-cleaned oyster shell and a small pearl, inserting the positive needle into the oyster shell. The negative needle was inserted into the pearl. Both needles were insulated from the other, a meter and variable resistor used as required. This was to lead to an important discovery how the body calcium could be used in reducing arthritis.

All of the connections located outside the glass jar, we filled the jar with distilled water in a solution of one to five percent sodium chloride and salt water. We turned on the switch for power and in a few days we could see the positive-connected oyster shell was dissolving. The calcium salts of the oyster were passing through the water solution, and the pearl was growing with the dissolved calcium from the shell. Small holes appeared in the oyster shell. The pearl and the oyster shell were hanging about three inches apart by threads in the jar with insulation as required.

What is important here is the similarity of body function. Calcium was dissolved using electrical current through a saltwater solution and transferred to another location, in this instance a pearl. This was further proof that bone calcium in the human body can be transferred from one location to another as needed since human blood is slightly saline in nature. What does this mean when arthritis is present? In those types of arthritis where calcium has increased, this buildup of calcium could be dissolved and removed to another point. Or it could be dissolved to enter the bloodstream and body fluids and be absorbed or eliminated. However, this would require a certain amount of surgery. Could applied magnetic fields externally, without surgery, accomplish the same desired result?

Since magnetism is a natural energy, and the human system has natural energy, if magnetic energy can heal a human injury it must be compatible with the natural energy of the human system. This we have found to be correct.

The negative energy of a magnet is similar to the negative healing energy of the body. The positive energy of a magnet is similar to the positive strengthening energy of the body.

Negative and Positive Energy Necessary

In our earlier book, *Magnetism and Its Effect on the Living System,* we have charted the voltages of the positive and negative energies in the human body. These energies are present throughout the body in a constantly flowing current. As our earlier published work has proved, when the natural balance of these energies is out of balance, that is when illness or disease occurs. The danger sign is always an increase above normal in negative energy at the location of injury. This occurs from a broken bone, infection, cancer or any other injury or illness.

The human system generates a higher amount of negative energy to aid a location of energy not in balance. The energy generated may not be sufficient to cure the imbalance. The natural way to aid this natural imbalance would be an added supply of the needed natural energy, as drugs, chemicals, or surgery all have side effects and are not reliable in all situations. Any responsible medical man or scientist will tell you that drugs, chemicals, surgery, do not "cure." Such procedure only arrests or controls a situation, hopefully, allowing the body's own natural energies to "cure" the problem.

Besides negative energy from a magnet, why not negative energy from another person for healing? This is what occurs in the effective laying on of hands. Not only negative healing can be applied but also the positive strengthening energy. We will explain this in more detail in the following chapters, as well as how you can better generate your own healing and strength-giving energy. We have already stated that faith with calm sincerity and a better understanding of your natural energy will aid your mind and body in the ability and use of your natural energy. You will better generate your energy. The use of magnetic healing energy externally from a magnet or from healing hands, if effective, is far more natural than drugs or chemicals for healing and relieving pain. Drugs and chemicals will upset, and radiation therapy will damage, healthy cells that are needed to defend the injury or illness.

Consider that with the needles, pins and flashlight battery procedure, both energies, positive and negative, are used together. The energies of a magnet can be used for a separate effective positive or negative use as desired. When both positive and negative magnetic energy is used for healing, such as bone regrowth, they are still separated in near relation for maximum effect of each energy to the desired areas of healing. Laying on of hands can be used in this same manner by the near relation separation and use of the desired energy.

Considering that the energies of healing hands can affect the human system similarly to the energies of a magnet, then what has our research further shown that can be accomplished with magnetic energies on animals and willing human subjects?

Our research indicates that the North pole Negative energy directed externally to an abnormal buildup of calcium, such as in forms of arthritis, will, over a period of time, in daily applications from weeks to months, slowly dissolve calcium that is not normal in bone growth.

The South pole Positive magnetic energy applied externally acts to expand, give strength and improve the circulation of the blood. Our publication *The Magnetic Effect* gives many more detailed applications, with type of magnet, strength of energy used and time and frequency of application.

It may be of interest for you to know that human and animal skulls are of a bone composition totally different from the rest of the body's bony structure. Modern science continues to cut and drill openings in the skull to remove growths and pressures on the brain such as tumors. After the operation implants of steel, nontoxic metals or plastics, are used to fill the opening in the skull. Even the ancient physicians who performed operations of the head more than a thousand years ago had no knowledge of this difference in bone construction. In our research we have discovered that the removed section or part of a skull ground into powder can be made into a cement that will fill the skull opening. This same composition of bone will knit and form to grow and cover the opening by natural body functions.

The Biomagnetic Nature

All performance of the body and its many parts and systems is bioelectrical, electrochemical and biomagnetic in Nature. Man is a walking, talking generator of thousands of different frequency vibrations of activity always in motion. Negative and positive energies are generated by the living system when in need. Ability to perform in the use of either energy will determine the overcoming of illness and disease and your very survival in your society.

4

The Healing Power of Your Hands

Natural healers use different effective methods. We have had the pleasure of knowing natural healers from all parts of the world. Many from this country and foreign countries have visited our laboratory interested in our work with natural energy. We have made personal visits in this country and abroad to see the work of healers, watched a number of films on the subject, studied photographs and researched considerable documentation. We have applied our laboratory research to the information we obtained.

Natural healing by the laying on of hands is a fact subject to proof. Wherever your location while reading this book you are not far from a recognized healer who may have assisted medical persons in their healing of patients. Natural healing has, in some areas, moved into the hospitals where the healer works together with the physician. There are also many effective healers in many different religious groups.

Some healers use both hands while others use one hand at a time. Many do not touch another person's body in any way, although they may place their hands near the sufferer and move their hands in circular or up-and-down motions. Each method as developed by the practitioner can be effective. Although we are somewhat similar we are not exactly the same in Nature. An effective healer adopts the methods that his or her investigations have proved best for desired results. We have found that most healers use a number of methods we have proved to be successful in our laboratory research. This also applies to well-known healers of history in many civilizations from the information we can obtain. What can be reproduced, over and over again, with desired results, is proof enough.

The scientific community demands reproducibility as proof to establish a Law. It is encouraging to see scientists considering in this day and age the possibility of natural healing, and some who profess their acceptance openly. In this chapter we will give more evidence for the acceptance by reproducibility.

Since more women are now entering into medicine and all fields of science we shall continue to see increasing success in the practice and acceptance of the laying on of hands. Women are generally more sensitive in scientific undertakings than men to the needs of the human race. A woman has an instinctive God-given natural ability for attending the ill, coupled with her experience in the care of the young. There are always exceptions to any personal generalization. Generally, the female of the species has sensitivities that man lacks, or has not developed, to the degree of the woman. This seems the rule for all living species, granting a few notable exceptions. The female of the species in their sensitivities can be the most kind or most deadly of all living creatures on the Earth. The nonbearing of a child seems not to lessen this sensibility.

Would you as a woman or a man make the best natural healer? Women are stronger and more knowledgeable in the human sensitivities. Man is stronger in physical strength, yet some studies show women can endure more than men. We have been asked many times if man's strength could make him more effective than the woman. What do our laboratory tests show?

1. Man's hands measure a greater normal amount of bioelectrical energy than a woman's hands.
2. Hands of women healers with less normal bioelectrical energy recordings have performed more effectively than men healers with greater energy recordings.
3. The greater amount of recorded normal energy in the hands does not by itself make the most effective healer.

We believe that man's strength gives him added power to make him the most effective. It is not the normal energy available as much as the energy that can be generated—and directed with a proper working of mind and body. Also, man, with greater physical strength, applying a known electromagnetic thesis, would tire more quickly in applying his available energy. Woman's energy would not weaken as quickly as man. Their more gentle, calm and sincere approach, would aid in a longer performance, and time of healing can be more important than amount of energy normally available.

4. Women can by concentration and practice gener-

ate in their hands equal or more bioelectrical biomagnetic strength than in the hands of men.

If the woman generates equal or more energy than the man she is then subject to the same outward flow of human magnetism. She would then experience weakness as the man from the results of effective healing. Yet the woman, with a built-in reserve of lower power that man does not possess, would not generally become as weak as the man. Circumstances seem to balance out one another. It would appear that both the man and the woman can be equally as effective as natural healers.

In work of this nature the ifs, buts, howevers, exceptions, can hardly be completely mentioned without a longer treatise than we intend in this presentation. One more point should be mentioned. Anyone who researches natural healing can point to a time in history or in the present when an effective natural healer did not keep himself in what could be called "good mental and physical condition." Also, you will find healers who do not seem to become weak after effective healing. These persons believed or did not believe in their energy from the grace of God. Based on our research in this matter, with due consideration of all the available factors, we stand on the following point.

5. You will be a better effective healer if you keep yourself in good physical and mental health with a calm sincerity that your natural energy flows from God.

How can we better identify the energies in the hands of men and women that appear to affect relief to the suffering? As a result of careful examinations, tests and recordings, we have discovered that the inside finger areas and the palms of the hands have two different types of energies on their surfaces.

THE RIGHT HAND: The palm, inside finger surfaces, inside parts of the fingertips, contain POSITIVE voltage. Magnetism and electricity are present, as in Nature; they can not exist separately. Here we have energy similar to that in the South pole of a magnet and to that energy found in the positive pole of a single-cell flashlight battery.

THE LEFT HAND: The palm, inside finger surfaces, inside parts of the fingertips, contain a NEGATIVE voltage. Both magnetism and electricity are present. The energy is similar to the energy in the North pole of a magnet and in the Negative pole of a small flashlight battery. We emphasize and stress the importance here.

RIGHT HAND PALM POSITIVE

LEFT HAND PALM NEGATIVE

You can see how our research in magnetism gives interesting breakthroughs and similarities in the laying on of hands. Reviewing similarities here, which hand would you use to relieve pain? When the North pole of a magnet, under proper use, is applied to a painful area the pain is reduced. With continued applications the pain is sedated, and with further use as indicated the arrest is complete. Other factors are considered in the use of a magnet, but for brevity this is the Law. It is the LEFT hand palm that acts in the same manner as the NORTH pole of a magnet to reduce and arrest the condition of pain. The palm and inner surfaces of the fingers have the similar power of energy, the NEGATIVE power.

What is the general Law for the other hand? What is the general Law of a magnet? The RIGHT hand palm presents a POSITIVE energy as the SOUTH pole of a magnet to promote strength, expand, give encouragement. Two more important Laws to remember.

RIGHT HAND STRENGTH

LEFT HAND REDUCES

Let us here consider some questions you may already be pondering.

QUESTION: Would you place the RIGHT hand palm against a painful area?

ANSWER: No. Positive energy of the RIGHT hand encourages strength. Applying strength to pain will increase the pain. This is in part due to the sensitivity of the nerves that would act to send more pain impulses to the brain receptor areas.

QUESTION: What hand palm would you place on the painful area?

ANSWER: The LEFT hand palm with the negative energy, as the similar negative energy in the North pole of a magnet will reduce sensitivity of pain with a sedating effect.

QUESTION: If a subject was very weak, what hand palm would you place on the weakened area?

ANSWER: Apply the South pole positive energy for strength. This would be the RIGHT hand palm. Do not apply to weakened area if pain is present.

QUESTION: Can both hands be used at the same time?

ANSWER: Yes. The RIGHT palm increases strength and the LEFT palm would sedate pain.

QUESTION: Does one energy cancel out the other energy?

ANSWER: No. Each separate energy will have its own effect, flowing from one hand to the other as energy flows from positive to negative terminals of a battery. Here you are using a total energy application.

QUESTION: Does the LEFT hand palm weaken the system by arresting strength?

ANSWER: This would depend on the interpretation of "weaken." The North pole Negative energies of the LEFT hand act to slow down and sedate to a good degree any activity in the area of application. The Negative energy lowers the pain threshold by lowering the sensitivity of the nerve endings.

QUESTION: But I am left-handed. Would this make a difference. Would my left hand have positive energy?

ANSWER: Our research has shown the LEFT hand palm is still NEGATIVE if you are primarily left-handed. Lower animals of this Nature also show no difference.

QUESTION: Energy and strength go together. If the left hand palm and fingers do not give strength, how can you say you still have energy?

ANSWER: There is energy and strength given from the LEFT hand palm and fingertips but it is not the kind that would encourage physical strength. The same is true with the North pole negative energy of a magnet.

The result is a "cleaning effect" instead of a "strength effect."

An analogy would be breathing negative air into the lungs. Negative charged particles of air called negative ions act to clean away positive charged particles in the atmosphere. Air that you breathe is approximately 75% nitrogen and 25% oxygen. Oxygen carries a negative charge. That is why applying oxygen is beneficial to an ill person. There is a cleaning effect produced. After the cleaning effect has progressed, the body's positive and negative energies more in balance, the system's own natural energies will give that stronger feeling of strength. It will be a calm strength of assurance, not a physical strength of dominance. Sufficient negative energy will arrest many types of viruses and bacteria that carry a positive charge.

In our research we have found that negative charged air can arrest many forms of disease. Oxygen, as a negative charged gas, acts in this manner, reducing the activity, life span, ability to reproduce of viruses and bacteria. In the balance of Nature, negative energy is vital to man, lower animals and plants in the environmental atmosphere.

Plants, vegetables and grass respond and exist more successfully in abnormal wet or dry conditions in a negative-charged environment. This is similar with man and the lower animals.

When man, lower animals and plants, experience a positive-charged atmosphere, they initially react more strongly, but prolonged exposure will encourage undesirable effects. Our work with the positive and negative magnetic energies on biological systems has shown that specific time periods of application are desirable. For example, in using magnetic energy on tomato seeds for increased protein and crop yield, 12 minutes exposure was preferable for optimum results rather than 15 minutes or longer. Our published works on animal research are definite in this regard. Another example you experience is the atmosphere changes on an approaching thunderstorm with its positive-charged environment. After the storm's activity has passed you should feel more relieved in the less positive-charged atmosphere.

QUESTION: All this is well and good. I can see the difference between the two hands. Can you tell me more about using both hands together for natural healing?

ANSWER: We have mentioned that electricity passes from the positive terminal of a battery to the negative terminal of a battery. This is a Law, and it applies when you place both hands on or near a person, animal or plant. Depending on your hands' location on the subject or near the subject, a current is now flowing through that subject or over the surface of its form, from the RIGHT hand position to the LEFT hand position. We call this a total energy application.

Many scientists claim that energy applied to the body passes around and over the skin surface and not through the skin or body. This may be true in some circumstances but not from the view of a total energy effect. If the energies of the hands basically followed the skin surfaces between the applied hands, the effects are to the entire body area not just the skin surfaces. Our research with magnetic energies show the energies travel into the body, and if the magnetic strength is sufficient, will leave the body after penetration, and continue.

Theories or Facts

In our applied research we are practical not theoretical scientists. We try to eliminate theory in our laboratory work by results that can be reproducible over and over again. This being so we consider we have truth not theory. We have found the RIGHT hand palm and inner surfaces of the fingers have a strengthening effect. The LEFT hand palm and inner finger surfaces have a sedating, soothing, cleaning, reducing effect. The use of both hands gives a total effect of both these energies.

5

Total Hand Energy, Brain Reaction, ESP

Any attempt to limit a Natural energy is useless. As we are imperfect in our progression with Nature that is all perfect in peace and order, we may narrowly construe any natural occurrence no matter how true we may be. Our knowledge will not be total comprehension. Our progression will, however, be more with truth and more with Nature.

QUESTION: Are the energies in the back of the hand the same as in the frontal palm and inner surfaces, and, if not, what is the difference?

ANSWER: The energies on the back of each hand are opposite to the energies on the front of each hand.

RIGHT HAND PALM POSITIVE

RIGHT HAND BACK NEGATIVE

And, with the left hand we have the same distinction.

LEFT HAND PALM NEGATIVE

LEFT HAND BACK POSITIVE

Each hand has both types of energy, positive and negative. This is an emphasis of another Law of Nature.

Positive energy and negative energy exist together. They cannot be separated but they can be arranged in near relation for a singular effect. There can be a preponderance or imbalance but there will be a near relation equaling effect.

Each hand, as each magnet, has both poles of energy. Each pole of energy produces a different effect. Therefore, each pole energy is a different form of energy.

As you would use the LEFT hand PALM you could use the BACK of the RIGHT hand for the same effect. A mother does this when she places the back of her right hand against her baby's brow to test for a temperature. Whether the mother is aware or whether this is a natural, normal inborn instinct could be prolonged discussion. This natural test for temperature is also practiced in the lower animals and not confined to the female in any species.

BACK OF THE HEAD POSITIVE

FRONT OF THE HEAD NEGATIVE

Here we have these two energies existing together in near relation. How do these energies on the head react to the hand energies? Our discoveries in this regard with electrical currents on the head were published in 1936. There is a similarity between the effects of electrical currents and the effects of hand energies.

If you place your RIGHT hand palm in back of the lower part of the head, and the LEFT hand palm against the frontal part of the head, this will enforce the natural energies of the head. The result will be an increase in strength and feeling of well-being. If you reverse the process, RIGHT palm positive to front of head negative, LEFT palm negative to back of head positive, there is a disturbing effect that lowers the efficiency of the brain. Remember, this is the use of hand and body energy of normally low voltage. What happens when the energy is increased to the head?

We used animals in our laboratory as test patients. We always take the upmost precautions never to injure our animals in any test. A small metal plate was placed on the foreheads and backs of their heads connecting the plates to a small battery of about 20 volts. A meter and suitable rheostat in series allowed adjustment of power going to the plates. Applying positive energy to the back plates, negative energy to the front plates, the animals became more alert and happy in playful activity. What happened when we suddenly reversed this higher energy to the head?

A switching system was used that could suddenly change the positive to negative and negative to positive. When this change was made the animals went limp into a state of unconsciousness. Russian scientists, researching with electrical currents to the brain, discovered this in the 1950s. They call it "Electro Sleep." This process is now used in this country under highly controlled research for placing a person who is to undergo surgery into a deep sleep. This removes the need to introduce drugs or other sedating methods during an operation. On a slow return of the normal voltages of the brain, the person awakens with no experience of the operation.

Electro sleep requires an increased amount of voltage and current controlled exactly, while the normal energy of the hands is much lower. However, the hands do have sufficient currents to relieve tensions and provide a sense of well-being as demonstrated in our research and by many natural healers.

ESP and the Third Eye

Extrasensory perception discussions invariably consider the center front of the forehead. This area is generally referred to as "the third eye." The evidence is strong that "the third eye" area of the brain is an important sensitive area.

In our research with this area of the brain we have found that applying negative energy to this location will increase ESP sensitivities. The North pole of a magnet for no longer than ten minutes has increased the mind's sensitivities. We found on human subjects that energy no higher than 300 gauss for periods only 3 to 5 minutes quite effective.

The LEFT hand PALM or BACK of the RIGHT hand on this location for 30 minutes has shown increase in ESP abilities, more ease of concentration and calmness in deliberation. The opposite procedure, the South pole of a magnet or the Positive energy of a hand makes the mind more active, but less calm and sensitive. Remember that the negative energy has strength but it is a calming inner strength not resembling physical strength.

Negative Energy Relieves Stress

Our chapter seven will more fully cover stresses in our societies, you, and healing energy. It is here important to consider that the negative energy on the third eye location does relieve to some degree what could be called the stresses and strains of civilization. There is less concern, worry, doubt to a problem that seemed evident. It is as if a weight had been lifted from your mind. In relieving stresses and strains imposed from man's structure of societies you are functioning more with the natural energies of your system. In this manner you are with strength from the use of negative energy, as you have moved more to your inner natural strength.

Positive Energy Increases Stress

The stimulation effects of South pole magnet energy on the brain can be unsafe and upset the natural mental activities. The hands, with less energy, generally, than magnets, are a safer means of soothing (Negative Energy) or strengthening (Positive Energy). A degree of caution is advised in the use of positive energy on the head.

At this point in our presentation we have given a basic understanding of the natural energies in your hands. Perhaps you already had this understanding from your inner Nature. Pause for a few minutes and consider calmly. Do you find it not difficult to believe what we have said is the truth in as far as we have explained? We will next give you a discovery from our research that has deep and profound significance.

The Closed Loop

Clasping the hands together in prayer is as old as history. Man would reach his arms to the heavens in wonder. Then he proceeded to clasp his hands together in prayer above his head. In cultures of present societies praying hands are generally in a clasped position over the mid-chest or lower stomach. Our research now establishes the clasping together of hands, in the field of electromagnetic physics, as a "closed loop" or a "closed circuit." Energy then flows through this circuit from the right hand palm positive to the left hand palm negative. Again we see the ancients in our history knew what they were doing. They used this position of the hands to give strength to the system as well as for prayers and meditation.

Supporting this ancient belief, when a test tube of an enzyme is placed between the palm of the right and left hand, after one to two hours, there is a rise in the enzyme activity. We will discuss this further in chapter eight. Generally, an enzyme is a living substance found in plants and animals, including man.

This test has been accomplished in a number of research laboratories, reproduced time and time again. Many scientists still refuse to pay any serious attention to this reproducible occurrence that has proved to be true.

In the same regard, the great majority of scientists today believe that you cannot change water. The truth of the matter is that you can change the hydrogen bonding in water. You can change water. This has been accomplished by natural healers under laboratory conditions, as well as with the use of magnetic fields in a number of research laboratories.

Your praying hands will strengthen your entire system. There is a real invisible rainbow of energy in your hands and in the hands of all men, women and children in the world today.

Why not offer a prayer before the laying on of hands? This will give you a feeling of added strength by closing the circuit of energies flowing through your system. Prayer, one of the greatest powers we possess, with the positioning of your hands in prayer, will increase your healing effectiveness. In this day and age to state that only a few possess these healing energies is incorrect. With NO EXCEPTION we all possess these natural energies, as do all the lower animals, and with calm sincerity they can be generated to help yourself and others in comfort and relief.

6

Positive Effects of Concentration with Faith

Concentration without Faith in natural healing is like having charity without love. For the most effective natural healing Faith is a necessary prerequisite. Concentration and Faith together, with calm sincerity, will generate increased natural energy in The Rainbow in Your Hands. You know this is truth. If you have not found this answer in your inner self you must try again to listen and to receive. It may take practice but this answer will never fail you, if you listen and receive with sincerity. Concentration acts to increase the mind's attention to a thought, an idea, a pain or an ache. You have focused with your natural energy. As you would focus on an injury you can focus on Faith.

In our lifetimes we have all bruised our hands, fingers, other parts of our body. Automatically, our attention is concentrated to that point of injury. You have a built-in alarm system with a silent bell that rings your attention to pain. You are placed on alert with a message sending SOS that you are in distress. You are called upon to do something to relieve the area in distress.

You have a built-in inner strength waiting for you to generate. Many of us never call upon this strength until the alarm bell rings. You do not need an alarm or injury to awaken your inner Nature. It is present whenever you wish to listen and receive. There never has and never could be in the history of the world a human being without this inner power. Concentration with Faith gives positive effects to natural healing.

You have noticed that concentration on an injury increases pain that is present. This is a natural occurrence as your mind's sensitivity has been enforced. Concentration on any part, section or area of your body enforces nerve sensitivity at that location. This in turn upgrades the nerve sensitivity to the brain receptors. You feel and know more than you did before concentration.

It is difficult to fix your attention on a part of your body that is not injured when pain is present. Still, most of us have done this many times. If you can focus your attention from your pain the nerve sensitivity to your brain will not increase the pain of your injury. If you can do this then you can focus your attention on Faith. Do not miss the great difference between Faith and Hope.

Faith and Hope Are Different

A person can sit in a chair and hope but this does not get to the problem. Hope is like give me, give me, give me, without giving anything in return. You can hope something constructive will happen to relieve or aid whatever it may be, but Faith is totally different. Faith means you know what can be done will bring about results. You know this with your very being. Faith is the knowledge there exists a greater power that will assist you if you in turn act to assist yourself. To simply sit and hope is not going to get the job accomplished. Faith and your will to accomplish will aid your prayers to come true, and this is the great difference between Hope and Faith to any outcome that you face.

For example, the LEFT hand palm presents a negative biological energy that can be used to sedate and soothe. This energy will add to a person's own negative energy the body had sent to a painful area. In applying the laying on of hands you will enhance, improve and amplify your healing energy by concentrating on the LEFT hand with your inner power of Faith. You will do the same with the RIGHT hand application. You will be drawing on your inner power of energy that will flow through your positive hand. The effects of either hand will be positive effects that you can see are working. Your mind and body will function in an upsurge of power. Once you have this experience you will never forget, and you will want the experience again. It is there when you concentrate with Faith in a manner no other means can fulfill.

Faith Is Power

Faith is energy in motion. You will generate your energy with Faith. Dr. Stanley Dean, M.D., psychiatrist with the University of Miami in Florida, states, "Science and Religion are fraternal twins that soon are to be united." This statement has been praised as much as it has been discounted. As scientists we have to be honest with you that the more we research natural energies the more respect and belief we have in God. We will have criticism since we see no difference in our discoveries between Science and Nature, although all religions of human societies are about Nature.

It is accepted science that all energy is motion. You can tap this energy and put it to work for yourself and others. You can concentrate with Faith and strengthen these abilities with prayers. You will then reflect confidence and security in your appearance. As scientists we would say you have become more with Nature.

Confidence Is Natural Healing

Having Faith and confidence is reflected in your face. It is "catching" by all those around you. Others feel your confidence from your energy as you feel this energy you are generating. This is a two-way spiritual strengthening between an ill person and a person expressing confidence in helping that person. You will be more effective in the laying on of hands and with others in your company. Science has proved that thought waves travel great distances. It has been proved that you can affect others with your thoughts. Our discoveries have proved these waves of energy travel in both directions, instantaneously, at the same time. As you think so will you affect others and yourself. Your confidence will express assistance to others with The Rainbow in Your Hands. If you are not confident you will reduce your healing energies and hinder others from receiving your energies. Concentration with Faith will increase your confidence. You will be more effective in the laying on of hands.

7

Today's Stresses, You, and Healing Energy

Many scientists are seeking answers to the cause, prevention and arrest of stress. The modern societies of today, most researchers agree, increase the presence of mental and physical stress resulting in illness, disease and death. It is well documented that much of heart illness and disease is due to stress. Research indicates many of man's illnesses are increased, if not caused, by stress. The human system is a delicate balance of natural energies. Any imbalance if not corrected will hinder your effectiveness in natural healing.

The World Is Much with Us

In these days of modern living great strife has been applied by political men and women and rulers of many nations, seeking to alter events in the world. Never have we been more conscious that some far-removed event can shape our lives. Man is ever changing his world, and we know these changes are not always peaceful. Man strives with whatever means are at his disposal to force his plans of improvements, whether or not they are allowable by the Master Plan of Nature. The damage to our environment that supports our very existence is now evident from the misuse of Nature.

We live in stress of new announcements that endanger our survival. Confidence in world leaders, governments, political activities, politicians has declined. Changing moral practices, economic woes, political and social disorders, if not immediately personal, bombard through mass communication of radio, newspapers and television. Facing every day additional stress upon his life and security, man is in increasing numbers returning to God. He is praying for strength and guidance to face this changing world. If The Rainbow in Your Hands can give you assistance and confidence in the truth of Nature and its power to combat imbalance and unnaturalness, your authors have accomplished their objective. Your mental and physical imbalances can be improved by an understanding of your natural energies and their effective use. The Secrets of Nature belong to God, but those that are revealed belong to All.

A world authority on stress, consulted by world governments, industrial and scientific leaders, wrote your senior author, "I have been following your work now for sometime." Dr. Hans Selye, M.D., medical practitioner and scientist from Montreal, Canada, is the author of a recent excellent book entitled *Stress Without Distress*. Dr. Selye had read our previous scientific books and was interested in our research on stress by the electromagnetic effects on man. Dr. Selye has advised that information we furnished to him will be used in his work. Your senior author has dedicated the past 40 years of his life researching the effects of energies, natural and man-made, on living systems. Research, as any worthwhile task, can be a tiring ordeal. A scientist can never anticipate if his work will be successful and, if successful, if it will be accepted by the scientific community. It seems at times more emphasis is based upon the college tie and degrees than accomplishments. Since we don't dwell on our degrees and prefer to remain independent in our research, we have encountered opposition from some accepted scientific organizations. We prefer to remain the way that we are. The science magazine *Industrial Research*, August 1975, in their editorial states, "Only a few important inventions of the past 40 years have originated in corporate labs . . . an almost-endless list of relatively recent inventions which were started in independent research, although most of them later were developed by large corporations. A small sample of these includes computers, radar, microwave technology, jet engines, inertial guidance, Xerography, instant photography, color photography, fiber optics, optical character readings, and the Wankel engine."

Our credentials are experience and research in living the science we have chosen to explore, obtaining facts that can be reproduced. We feel our abilities are not only based on our many years in practical laboratory research, sociological and scientific investigations, but also on the fact that many national and international authorities seek our counsel to confer on these subjects. Since our discoveries touch upon the basis of all human knowledge, as we believe and are advised, we are always supplementing our research by our further education in man's affairs outside our laboratory. As we have authorities seeking our advice we seek the advice of others. We have learned much from others as we hope others have learned much from us.

A change in our policy the last several years has been to release more of our work to you, the general public. We believe that knowledge in the hands of you the people is more important than in the hands of a few. Too often bureaucracies of authority limit, ignore and delay facts of scientific importance to the people's happiness and survival. We have also become more conscious the past few years that many of our scientific discoveries are being restricted by a number of scientists who believe and accept our work. Although we can understand the reluctance of those trained in the old school of science to publicly support new reproducible facts that go against one's book and educational learnings, we must deplore the lack of dissemination in any new discoveries that can assist mankind, including other scientists in their research.

We are here reminded of a former Nobel Prizewinner who has released his "theory" on the electromagnetic nature of cancer. This dedicated scientist, not knowing of our research in arresting cancer with magnetic energy, wrote to us that his concept on the "electron" of cells did not include magnetic effects on cells. Here we wish to state that our work involves many aspects of natural energies on the human and lower animal systems, including plants, seeds and other living systems. Our work on stress has also included research on water, gases and solids, as the study of electromagnetic energies includes all things of Nature whether natural or man-made.

Living with Stress

You are bombarded with hundreds, if not thousands, of electromagnetic stresses every day that are not Natural to your system. Can you then more readily understand why we are having more mental and physical breakdowns in our societies? Much of these man-made stresses are unknown, and their dangers when suspected are in many instances not properly investigated, due in part to the vested interests in our societies that would have to adjust their interests, if proof of these dangers became too well known to the general public.

There are thousands of radio, television and shortwave stations, high frequency microwaves, telegraph, telephone signals, and even telephone calls, exposing your body, brain and organs every day of your existence. Yes, your telephone is made in a manner that exposes you to electromagnetic energies passing to your brain. Each time you place your telephone to your ear a strong magnetic energy is affecting you. Here is a discovery that we believe you, the people, should know. From the hundreds of telephones we checked, all radiated a positive South pole magnetic energy of sufficient strength to penetrate your skull into your brain. How have the government agencies missed this fact? Yes, you certainly should heed the phone company suggestions to "keep your phone calls short." Our published research that is reproducible fact indicates your telephone receiver could be a health hazard. Shouldn't the government protective agencies, the Surgeon General, order a label to be placed on each and every telephone radiating this positive energy, "WARNING—THE SURGEON GENERAL HAS DETERMINED THAT THE USE OF THIS TELEPHONE MAY BE DANGEROUS TO YOUR HEALTH." If you can obtain a magnometer from a scientific supply company or other source you can measure this magnetic energy on your own telephone.

Did you know that electric shavers produce alternating currents of electromagnetic energies that pass into the head? And, what about electric toothbrushes where these energies penetrate into your mouth and throat? Our publication *Magnetism and Its Effects on the Living System* will give you more information on these vibratory frequencies of electromagnetic energies.

Government authorities are now warning about micowave ovens. The doors and other parts may become worn, permitting high frequency alternating energy to escape to your harm. Electric hair dryers with electrical sparking motors send out many forms of high and low frequency electromagnetic energies. Your dentist may have a "new device" that cleans your teeth with high frequency vibratory waves. We are continually in our man-made socieities developing more and more electronic hazards to our health. You are not confined to only the natural electromagnetic influences on your system from the earth, air, atmosphere and from distant space, but you are daily influenced by man-made vibrations affecting your natural balance of energies. We hope this has revealed to you the importance of keeping yourself in good mental and physical condition, with strong Faith, to direct your healing ability to yourself and others.

In our research on the healing effects of the hands it was necessary to construct a "Shielded Room" that to a good degree prevented the interference from the multitude of natural and man-made electromagnetic energies. Remember that the hands normally contain a very minute part of energy compared to a small flashlight battery. In this manner we determined that each hand contains an important natural complex of energies, perhaps thousands of modulated energies, and many unknown at this time. Remarkable were our findings that without the shielding protection in our usual surroundings, with all the man-made electromagnetic interferences, the human energy system can still generate effectively with The Rainbow in Your Hands. Our research shows a definite link between the energies of a magnet's two poles and the energies in each hand of the human system. Our reproducible findings support the effects of the hand's energies on living systems.

Some additional factors to assist your healing abilities in avoiding stress when applying the laying on of hands are as follows:

1. Make contact by your hands with the other person.

2. Rub your hands together vigorously, bring them slightly apart, then almost together. Feel the energy in your hands.

3. Breathe in and out several times to assist in calming yourself, releasing carbon dioxide as you take in oxygen. This is an effective practice of some cultures in awakening your inner strength. Several minutes of deep breaths are very helpful to your Nature.

When you make direct contact with the other person the energy of the hands is not lost by the interference of other electromagnetic energies passing through or around your body. Some natural healers do not place their hands for contact. These healers could be more effective since a loss of energy is occurring. Air acts as an insulator to electric energy flow. However, the flow of magnetism is not prevented by this cushion of air. Yet there will still be a loss of available energy. In our work with magnetic energy we have found the greatest amount of energy near the magnet poles. The farther from the magnet poles the less strength recorded. This has also been recorded with the hands of healers.

No longer can the natural energies of the hands be doubted. In our next chapter we will present some outstanding discoveries by other scientists that support our presentation.

8
Independent Verification

Dr. Justa Smith has a doctor's degree in biochemistry. She is director of research at the Human Dimensions Institute, Buffalo, New York, and chairman of the Chemistry Department, Rosary Hill College in Buffalo. Her laboratory tests and findings give supporting evidence to the healing power of The Rainbow in Your Hands.

Before Dr. Smith investigated effects of the laying on of hands she had a scientific background of research into the effects of ultraviolet light and high magnetic fields on enzyme activity. She was assisted by Hungarian Army Colonel, retired, Oskar Estebany, an effective healer of The Rainbow in Your Hands. Colonel Estebany's work as a healer had previously been tested by Dr. Bernard Grad, McGill University biochemist in Montreal, Canada.

Dr. Grad's work showed that seeds would sprout faster, plants grow better and animals wounds hasten in healing by the use of "healing hands." These experiments were accomplished under controlled laboratory conditions. Colonel Estebany is a distinguished gentleman. During the Hungarian Revolt of October-November, 1956, medical facilities were scarce and often not available. Colonel Estebany went to the wounded, sick and ill, and applied the laying on of hands, relieving pain and suffering that was often under direct battlefield conditions.

In the tests by Dr. Smith, the enzyme Trypsin was placed in a solution in glass-stoppered test tubes and Colonel Estebany would hold them between his hands for one to two hours. All of the tests showed a significant increase of activity in the enzyme solution. Proper laboratory controls were used. A test tube containing an enzyme solution not treated showed no change in activity. To avoid a relation of body heat, the test tubes were maintained before treatment at the same temperature as Colonel Estebany's hands.

Why is increase in enzyme activity by human hands important? The apparent metabolic reactions of each human cell are catalyzed by specific enzymes. To this extent, enzymes are considered the brains of cells. It is believed that any disease or illness develops from the lack of activity or malfunctioning of enzymes. It would then appear that any change in cellular structure of disease or illness would require a change in the enzyme catalysts. Before Colonel Estebany applied his healing hands, Dr. Smith had damaged the speed of enzyme reaction between 60 to 70 percent less than normal by the use of ultraviolet light exposure. Laying on of hands restored up to 23 percent enzyme activity.

In Dr. Smith's research with magnetism she placed her test tubes of enzymes between the two poles of a magnet and this also recorded a rise in enzyme activity up to 10 percent. Our research with the separate poles of a magnet was not known to her, wherein the South pole magnet energy will increase enzyme activity more than 10 percent. Before we tell you about another group of important laboratory tests supporting The Rainbow in Your Hands, let us examine here some facts not presented in the experiments already mentioned.

1. Magnetism passes through glass. It will even pass through a sheet of lead. Lead is used in radiation laboratories to shield the workers from exposure. X rays will not pass through lead, nor will atomic energy. Magnetism will pass through lead with no loss of magnetic energy.

2. Electricity will not pass through a sheet of glass nor through the walls of a glass test tube. Glass is an insulator of electricity.

What has caused a change in enzyme activity in the glass-stoppered test tubes? It cannot be electricity in the hands of the healer since glass is an insulator of electricity. Was it human magnetism? We know that a magnet's energies will pass not only through the glass walls of a test tube but also through the enzyme solutions and hands, bones and flesh of Colonel Estebany, or any man, woman or child who would have held the test tubes.

Our previous published research, and the work of many other scientists, supports the well-established Law that magnetism and electricity are a combined energy. One energy cannot exist without the other energy. However, there is a distinct difference in applying this Law to human energies. For example, electricity from a battery is a form of power that is almost totally direct current. Human electricity, better said as human electricity and magnetism, electromagnetic, contains hundreds, even thousands, of alternating currents, voltages, of different frequency vibrations per second. When voltages and currents experience vibrations they are not true direct currents but are many different frequencies of energy.

Yes, we have Laws that work in our limited capacity to discover and understand. The more a discovery on the human system is revealing, the more it shows how little we know about Nature's Peace and Order, and the more doors that are opened for further discoveries. We are examining the energies in the hands and we find a remarkable combination of many energies. The energy generated each time the heart beats is found in the hands. The frequency vibrations are from 60 to 90 pulses every minute depending on the heart's usual condition. A muscle in movement, a limb activated, breathing occurring, presents energy emissions. The brain of man is a constant source of frequencies ranging from a few vibrations to millions of vibrations per second. Imagine the amazing discoveries to be made in this area since most of present research has been with the vibrations of the brain up to only 50 cycles per second. Each organ, each part, each segment, perhaps even each atom, in the human has its own vibration cycle, functioning with Peace and Order in a balance of Nature expressed in The Rainbow in Your Hands. Human magnetism must exist in the hands for their energies to pass through the walls of a glass test tube altering activity of living enzymes. Now we will tell you about some extraordinary laboratory experiments of the energy in your hands.

In our work with natural energies of Nature we meet many wonderful and dedicated persons in research activities. Two such persons are Dr. Robert N. Miller and Dr. Olga Worrall. Dr. Miller is an industrial research scientist for the Lockheed Corporation who is also active in the scientific investigation of healing hands. Dr. Olga Worrall is an internationally known healer recognized in many countries of the world. The best-selling book *The Gift of Healing* by Olga and her husband, Ambrose A. Worrall (Harper & Row, New York), was first published in 1965 and is still much in demand. A recent publication by Edwina Cerutti, *Olga Worrall, Mystic with the Healing Hands* (Harper & Row, New York), gives further insight into the experiences of this gifted woman.

In 1974 at Agnes Scott College, Atlanta, Georgia, Dr. Miller, Dr. Worrall, with Dr. Philip B. Reinhart, head of the Physics Department, Agnes Scott College, conducted experiments in the physics laboratory to determine if a healer's hands did emit measurable energy. The tests were successful and the results have been published throughout the world. This research was conducted under assistance from the Ernest Holmes Research Foundation.

A cloud chamber was used for the tests. This is a device in physics; for these experiments, the floor of the chamber was covered with a layer of methyl alcohol and placed on a flat block of dry ice. The liquid alcohol, in a closed volume of air, evaporates into the air in the chamber, forming a vapor. Charged particles of alpha and beta rays, passing through the chamber, ionize the air, and positive and negative ions show their travel. All this can be observed through the sealed glass chamber.

Dr. Worrall placed her hands near the sides of the chamber, concentrating on her energy flowing from her hands. Wave patterns developed that followed the direction of her hands. Changing hand positioning, the wave forms changed to her hands' location. Other experiments were conducted substantiating the conclusion that a healer's hands produce energy that can alter and stimulate cell activity. Generally not publicized as the healing hands experiments were other experiments at Agnes Scott College conducted with magnetism, that substantiated our discovery that magnetism and the energy in the hands of a healer are similar energies, with similar effects on living cells.

Dr. Worrall, as well as other gifted healers, as Olga says, "are always under scientific scrutiny." A number of outstanding scientists, under scientific controlled laboratory conditions, are finding from their tests with healers that something is there. We believe that something is human magnetism, that we have recorded in our studies on the human body, which is a basic energy of Nature, similar to the energy found in an ordinary magnet.

It would be too lengthy here to mention all the scientists in this research. One outstanding lady deserves great praise for her pioneering work, and that is

Dr. Thelma Moss, medical psychologist and assistant professor at UCLA's Neuropsychiatric Institute. This researcher has photographed the energy in the hands of Dr. Worrall and other healers. This is a photographic process that has been used to depict "changing colors" of energy in the practice of The Rainbow In Your Hands."

Did you know that the energy that lights your home and powers your washing machine can be found on the surface of your body? Yes, the normal house current vibrates at the rate of 60 times per second (60 cycles per second). Also recorded on your body system are the energies from fluorescent and incandescent lights, including percentages of ultraviolet, X rays and other charged ions of energy. When you realize that the hands of all humans possess these many electromagnetic vibrations of energy, you can understand that man is an electromagnetic, biomagnetic animal, existing with and among electromagnetic interferences from Nature and from man.

Here we would like to mention a few of our close friends that have helped our research in substantiating the importance of magnetism to man's Nature. The noted science writer Joseph F. Goodavge has introduced our work to many scientists throughout the world. His article of July 1964 in *Fate* magazine, entitled "Man, the Biomagnetic Animal," was excellent on the biomagnetic Nature of man. Dr. Frederick Doughty Beck of New Orleans has assisted us for many years, as has Dr. Ralph U. Sierra of Rio Piedras, Puerto Rico. Dr. Harold Brownlee, Oshawa, Canada, has assisted in our research of diagnosing illness with the two poles of a magnet. Recently, another dedicated researcher who worked with us has published a comprehensive work on the energies of man, Dr. Victor R. Beasley of the West Indies, the study entitled, *The Supersensitive Life of Man,* subtitled "Dimensions of Electro-Vibratory Phenomena" (University of the Trees Press, Boulder Creek, California). The publication was the thesis for Dr. Beasley's Ph.D. degree. Dr. Smith received her degree by her research and writings in this area of science. An increasing number of scientists are writing on the magnetic and electromagnetic effects of Nature.

The first book published on our work was by Dr. A. K. Bhattacharya, West Bengal, India, in 1970, *Magnet and Magnetic Fields* (Firma K.L. Mykhopadhyay, Calcutta). In 1956 we introduced the Science of Biomagnetics into the free clinics of India, with the assistance of Dr. Bhattacharya. We received acknowledgment from Prime Minister Gandhi for the many thousands in India who have benefited from this new understanding of Magnetism.

Dr. Leslie O. Korth, Tunbridge Wells, Kent, England, is a talented researcher and the author of a number of excellent books on the different arts of healing. Recommendation is here given on his book *Healing Magnetism* (1974, Thorsons Publishers Limited, Denington Estate, Wellingborough, Northamptonshire, England).

Another scientist of our acquaintance deserving noteworthy mention for his research in energy fields is George W. Meek, Ft. Myers, Florida. George's background was in industrial engineering. He now travels to many countries of the world researching, lecturing and writing on the natural healing talents of many persons. His photographs on Kirlian Photography and his films on the psychic healers of the Philippines are outstanding. His recent book *From Enigma to Science* (Samuel Weiser, Inc., New York, 1973) is a thorough treatise on the energies in natural healing.

The increased concern for our troubled natural environment, the realization that societies of our world have never been so close to annihilation, has focused additional attention upon understanding more of Nature, and magnetism is a basic energy to our understanding of Nature.

9

The Workings of Human and Animal Magnetism

Jean Jacques Rousseau, French philosopher of the eighteenth century, led a movement of "return to Nature." He moved to the countryside in a beautiful château with servants and luxuries and enjoyed and wrote of the beautiful splendor of Nature. Today we are going to the seashore, finding a retreat in the mountains, hunting, fishing, anything to remove ourselves from the fervor and haste of modern living. Nature is all around you. You do not need to take a retreat from your means of living to discover Nature. Nature is you. You need only to discover yourself, and you will be with Nature, and with God. All the beauties of God's works are to be found within your own being. Find these wonders and you will then naturally express them in your day-to-day existence.

In our book *Magnetism and Its Effects on the Living System*, we present in some detail the positive and negative energies that can be found in and without the living system. Negative energy is the control energy that acts to prevent a breakdown in your system. Your body generates, supplies and directs this form of electrical and magnetic energy during your entire physical life. Without this energy there would be no life. For example, in biological chemistry, oxygen has a natural negative electrical and magnetic charge. Oxygen cleans the blood and body fluids among its many benefits.

Our work with magnets has shown these natural energies affect the electrical and magnetic polarization of blood in the living system. The Nobel Prize-winner, Dr. Linus Pauling, in the 1930s discovered that blood, leaving the lungs and traveling throughout the body, slowly turns positive due, in part, to acquiring oxides and toxins in the blood. When the blood returns to the lungs it receives an oxygen bath produced in the lungs and changes back to a clean, negative, electromagnetic charge. Also, in the biomagnetic energies of the body, an acid is positive and an alkaline is negative.

The North pole negative energy encourages alkalines in the system; the South pole positive energy encourages acids in the system. Relating to your palm energy is the following similarity:

LEFT PALM ENCOURAGES ALKALINES

RIGHT PALM ENCOURAGES ACIDS

Furthering this similarity is the Law:

NEGATIVE ENERGY ENCOURAGES ALKALINE CONDITIONS

POSITIVE ENERGY ENCOURAGES ACID CONDITIONS

Human blood is slightly alkaline (negative in Nature and energy). It will remain alkaline (negative) until circulating through the body it turns slightly acid (positive). If blood were to remain even a low percent acid, the person or animal would become very ill, and most likely die as a result.

Remembering Dr. Pauling's discovery we should consider that the white blood cells, the white bacilli, are the soldiers that come to the aid of a damaged part of the body. They are always in reserve ready to defend against the invading enemy of bacteria and germs.

WHITE BLOOD CELLS NEGATIVE ENERGY

RED BLOOD CELLS POSITIVE ENERGY

These are active energy generations of blood cells, yet note this interrelation. The outside surface of each blood cell membrane has a negative charge while the inside center of each blood cell has a positive charge of energy. Interrelating the Laws of body energy to The Rainbow in Your Hands substantiates the healing powers of your hands.

LEFT HAND PALM HEALING ENERGY

RIGHT HAND PALM STRENGTH ENERGY

In the use of both hands, place the LEFT hand PALM where pain or swelling is located. Place the RIGHT hand PALM on the opposite side of the body part to increase the flow of strength. However, the LEFT hand PALM, or the BACK of the RIGHT hand, is the healing negative energy and, as such, should be considered foremost in relieving pain and discomfort.

Researching the natural healing art of the laying on of hands in many cases showed the use of the right palm on the opposite of the problem did not bring relief.

In an undertaking of this book's nature, as scientists, mention of the Russian scientists' research on natural energies is necessary. Since the word Science stands for knowledge, a research scientist should seek out knowledge where it may be obtained. In this respect any man, woman or youth who seeks knowledge on a subject is, in fact, a research scientist. The Russian research the last few years on natural energies is noteworthy in contribution to science. As we write this chapter we note that the authoritative American magazine *Physics Today* has recognized the Russian research with their issue of November 1975 devoted to Soviet Physics. First, we state here frankly that we disagree with the Russian interpretation of science. Generally, the Russian scientists will tell you that they "create." Our interpretation is that a scientist "discovers." Also, from our own experience, we are cautious in believing every claim of Russian scientists. For example, there has been tremendous publicity in scientific areas of a process attributed to the Russians called Kirlian Photography. This manner of photographing electrical energy of a charged body on a photographic negative film by the use of electrodes was developed in our laboratories in the 1930s. We still have a number of the old original photos from this research. However, the Russian scientists are making important breakthroughs in the extrasensory perception and transmission of thought information. Their work in nerve and muscle operation by artificial means is also outstanding.

Relating more specifically to human and animal magnetism, the Russian research indicates that the brain's extended range of frequency vibrations per second is far beyond what the remainder of the scientific world believes. They say the usual study of 1 to 50 cycles per second of the brain's energy does not account for the higher vibrations that may exceed up to and over 1,000,000 cycles per second. In this respect we have to agree.

We are on record to parapsychology foundations, societies and scientists that the accepted basis of possible thought transmissions could not operate in such a manner. The lower frequency of energy per second the more power necessary for the distance traveled by that energy. The higher frequency, the less power necessary, and the more distance the energy will travel, instantaneously. For example, a frequency of 20,000,000 cycles per second, 20 megacycles per second, can travel around the world and back to its starting point in less than a second of time. What this means, if we are correct, and our thesis is based on the known laws of electromagnetic physics, is a "new look" at the instruments presently in use in recording brain wave patterns. Cathode ray oscillographs, biofeedback and other computer instruments, have been designed to filter out higher frequencies to prevent interference with the lower readings. New pictorial display instruments should be designed to study the possible high frequency vibrations of the brain's natural energies. It is a scientific fact that the human brain functions as a receiving and transmitting station of energies. These energies are modulated (intermixed) with thousands of body frequencies and generated in The Rainbow in Your Hands.

Can the feet be used to heal? Could persons who have lost one or even both hands or arms heal with their feet? We can find no reason why these persons cannot be as effective in natural healing as persons equipped with hands and arms. The soles of the feet are larger than the hands and can be applied to more surface area. There is a greater amount of normal natural energy on the surfaces than in the hands. In laboratory tests we found the soles of the feet are highly receptive to a healer's hands. The science of applying healing hands to the soles of the feet is practiced throughout the world.

RIGHT FOOT SOLE POSITIVE ENERGY
LEFT FOOT SOLE NEGATIVE ENERGY

Thus, the techniques described in this book can be used by those with no arms or hands.

RIGHT FOOT SOLE STRENGTH ENERGY
LEFT FOOT SOLE HEALING ENERGY

Can the deaf and blind be effective natural healers? Certainly. There are healers of this Nature. Handicapped persons are endowed with God-given sensitivities not present in other persons. Their inner natural abilities have been more developed through their inner strength of Nature. They make excellent natural healers.

10
The Bionic Masterpiece of Nature

Man is the world's greatest living electronic, electromagnetic, biological, mechanical composite, the bionic masterpiece of Nature.

Man has a conscience of right or wrong. He can experience the results of his behavior and he can rely on his conscience as his guardian and his guide. The greatest writings of the world examine in detail the results of following this inner strength of Nature.

It is written that man has all the necessary things to provide him with a good and natural life, if he would learn of their existence and use them wisely. His hands and his strength can build. His mind can think and analyze. Through his God-given instinct of conscience he can guide his life and those of others. Nature has provided an environment for natural living if man will work with Nature and not work to destroy. Plants, trees and shrubs in our surroundings provide negative healing energy; the Sun provides warmth and light energy to encourage their growth. The leaves of all plants provide clean oxygen for man to survive. As falling leaves and vegetation die and decay, they mix with the soil, providing nitrogen for fertilizing foods, plants, trees, flowers and a necessary part of the air we breathe. These are but a few of the many wonders God provides for man and all living things.

Nature also acts to remove poisons from the air. Leaves and green vegetation breathe in carbon dioxide and breathe out oxygen. The attempts of societies in modernizing the world are destroying these very parts of Nature necessary for man's survival. Each seed that is planted, each flower, plant or tree you grow, will assist Nature in the attempt to provide man and all living things with their natural environment. The Rainbow in Your Hands expresses the greatness you hold in your hands, your minds, your very thoughts and inner strength, that you can direct toward a natural world. As the hands obey your mind and your desires, then place them to the use they were intended—with Nature—with God.

In the developments of modern science have come understandings about our world that all energy is a force of power continuously in motion. When this energy is applied there is always present an unseen counteraction. There is always a reaction that is in reverse direction of the applied force. Stop a minute and think about this. Consider the profound significance of this Law.

Energy of any form, type, whatever, always flows in this manner.

Energy Flows in Two Directions

When you apply the laying on of hands, or thought energies, what you are sending will return, and could give you far greater strength than you expressed.

Power Flows in Two Directions

This is not science fiction. This is scientific fact. It is knowledge, and it is Nature. The long-standing maxim that so you think so you are is true to the Laws of Nature.

Love is an example of the action and counter-action of universal Law existing in Peace and Order throughout universal knowledge. Our universe exists on Balance, one relation to another, one energy to another. Love has a balancing effect to Peace and Order. Hate is a heavy weight that upsets the balance of Life's pattern. Concentration with calm sincerity of your inner Nature of God's strength will assist your balance of energies. Your pain and suffering and that of others can be relieved with your understanding and applying what you know is true to Nature. It rests in your hands and the hands of all mankind the power to maintain a balance between the advancements in modern living and the Laws that Nature has provided for a natural environment.

Peace and Order Is the Balance

All living things in the known existence of mankind must abide by this predominant Law or ultimately perish.

Nature has provided plants, herbs, roots, leaves, barks, that will relieve pain and infection, disease and illness. Nature has provided the lower animals, as well as man, the inborn intelligence to seek and identify natural remedies. For example, have you ever watched a kitten, that you could see by its appearance and behavior was not well, go to an area of green grass and chew fluids from the grass leaves? Cats know that by doing this they will feel better. Their inborn intelligence provides the ability for them to see the way they should go. Did you know that the mouth saliva of animals has a negative healing energy charge? The natural way that animals clean themselves gives them a healing energy application against pain and infection.

When we examine the ancient and modern civilizations of man it appears that mankind has never had the built-in intelligence to survive with Nature as the lower animals. In ancient times man was forced by trial and error to learn what plants, barks, roots and herbs could be used to relieve suffering. As a more comfortable life was developed in the complex societies the knowledge of natural things seems to have disappeared. It then remained for the few that sought to rediscover Nature's ways to progress man's existence on this Earth. The destruction of the great library of knowledge at Alexandria when Caesar departed from Egypt cannot be measured in the loss to civilization. Ancient wonders and mysteries remain secret, revealed only to those who seek the answers in Nature's plan of Peace and Order. What glories of God are yet to be revealed are not imaginable. The few pitiful remnants of knowledge expressed in our daily behavior are frightening. Considering that a few hundred years ago our ancestors were well trained in natural healing and the use of natural vegetation, and looking at the knowledge today of natural healing, we wonder how so much could have been lost in such a short period of time in man's history. Man has become so self-centered and narrow-minded in his false pride of accomplishment that he is amazed when told he must depend on Nature to survive. His arrogance to God, his fellow humans, and to peaceful animal life, shows no bounds in ignorant behavior. He forgets that by the grace of God he is the bionic masterpiece of Nature.

It is heartening to see the many men, women and especially young persons, seeking ways and means to understand the natural Peace and Order of Nature. It is equally distressing to see the conduct of many mature men and women more concerned about their material accomplishments. In this modern civilization we struggle and strive to accomplish, only to find in many instances that we feel as though we did not exist. There is a mad race to escape one's self in bureaucracies of authority and direction, usually of our own design, and then we find too often we have missed the boat. We follow a treadmill of meaninglessness into oblivion.

No Person Escapes Himself

This is an impossible task that cannot be accomplished by the Nature of our being. You can make a good attempt at shutting out your inner Nature, and fooling others with your behavior as well as yourself, but you will not succeed. The inner sparks of Life within you bring to mind your own folly. If you continue in this behavior the result will be remorse, illness and death. To preserve your natural balance of energies you must listen to your inner strength of conscience with calm sincerity, then you will know and act accordingly.

We have presented a new scientific understanding of natural healing by the laying on of hands. We are not attempting to offer you medical advice nor turn you from your family doctor. We are scientists not medical doctors, and the laws of society are strict in who should give medical advice. As scientists, and as human beings, we present in this book ways and means by which you within yourself can discover the truth of what we say, for your self-help and the help of others. We also have the right to give our views that from our experience are for the best interests of Peace and Order to your Nature.

Are we losing that wonderful part of progression, the Family Doctor? Do we have the feeling and concern in the modern physician of today that existed in the bedside manner of our medical culture? Is medicine too busy, too expensive, and just too much medicine to swallow? We mean this in a definitely serious manner, not to criticize unfairly, only where criticism is due with just cause. Modern medicine is not in keeping with the human needs. We say this in all due respect to the many dedicated and wonderful persons in the medical arts. For whatever reason is suitable, it is a fact that the feeling and concern of the family physician are disappearing in the realm of civilization. Diagnoses are increasingly incorrect, as physicians continue to treat the effects and not the cause. Malpractice law suits are growing in number, and for all the excuses and fault-blaming on others, the fact remains that physicians are making more mistakes in our more advanced technology.

Perhaps we are also believing more that physicians, as well as lawyers, politicians, statesmen, are not above the Law, as we seek out the faults inherent in our conglomerated societies. The attitude of a physican that he knows it all, has no time for the elderly, considers a patient as only a 50 dollar fee or more, is unwanted in our day and age. Finally, we see honest and dedicated men of science who are not afraid to speak out against their fellow practitioner when wrong occurs.

A growing concern with hundreds of medical men we personally know, and as expressed publicly by some medical authorities, is the apparent lack of bedside manners on the part of those now entering into the practice of medicine. It is generally recognized that somehow in the struggle against disease and illness the physician must find more time and personal concern for the patient. Our educational system, in preparing young persons for higher education, is turning out increasing numbers of diploma-educated persons who cannot properly read and write basic English. As we seem to hurry ourselves in an escape from Nature, we also seem to discard in our societies the basic elements that have proved worthwhile, and in education the foundation of reading, writing and arithmetic has not been surpassed. What more of the basic values are we losing through education? When our elderly citizens, men and women, retire or reach the time they cannot do the work that has occupied their lives, they need that little extra time, that bedside manner, understanding, with a warm smile. They do not need and do not deserve the over professional attitudes much in evidence today.

If the older men and women had some basic understanding how they could better take care of themselves, this could remove a great amount of overload on the medical professionals. Such persons could, in fact, be as a nurse's aide to other mature citizens. More self-help is needed for the patient rather than the repeated slogan of go to the drugstore, get the prescription filled, and, if it doesn't work then come back and we will try something else. The Rainbow in Your Hands expresses the power all medical professionals hold in their hands to help the sick, the ill, the suffering men and women who come to them. We are supposed to be men and women who know what life is all about, but the truth of the matter is we live in the dark ages to Nature, in fear of the unknown, that can be opened to you in all its harmony of Peace and Order.

Most serious illnesses develop over a long period of time. They do not just happen. Preventive medicine requires only your desire and knowledge to help yourself. This is common sense for living. Medical men should instruct their patients more in how to take care of themselves, not carry on the practice of trying one medication after another, hopeful that one will work. Drugs and medicines relieve pain in some instances, but they do not arrest or cure a cause, only sometimes an effect. Healthy cells of the body are necessary to combat illness without the prolonged deadening by drugs and medicines. Preventive medicine should be the guide, for yourself and the medical practitioner. Nonsensible diets should be avoided. Fresh air, a balance between work and recreation, exercise and cleanliness, with nourishing foods, should be the prime concern of both patient and the physician. There is a Rainbow in Your Hands that can be used for your self-help if you but direct your mind and efforts. If you cannot look after yourself, you will not effectively assist others.

Laying on of Hands Is Natural

There are no drugs, no medicines and no surgery in the laying on of hands. While the natural healing science of laying on of hands is of vital importance in the healing arts, some will require more study and concentration than those who will perform more quickly. Looking at the total picture of natural healing as it applies to all of us, we all should learn as much about preventive medicine as we can. There are excellent sources for you in this regard and we will mention a few we have investigated and find worthwhile.

Many books are written on the proper care of the human system. We have not been able to find, in our opinion, any one book that offers a complete, sensible approach to preventive medicine for everyone, although there are a number of books that can be helpful to many in some areas of self-help. The books by the authoress Adelle Davis are very helpful in this regard. We would suggest you can help yourself in preventive medicine by finding a reputable natural health organization and following its literature, which is usually inexpensive to acquire. A number of these organizations have members who are professional doctors of medicine, osteopathy, naturopathy and chiropractic, as well as other professional persons, working together in the field of natural health and care of the living system.

One such organization is the National Health Federation, Post Office Box 688, 212 West Foothill Boulevard, Monrovia, California 91016. We came to know about this organization through a good friend of our acquaintance for many years who has devoted his life to lecturing and studying the human system, Dr. William A. Ellis. Connected with this organization is the talented film star Gloria Swanson, who has campaigned most of her life for vigorous health through natural methods, and is especially active in natural health against the use of dangerous chemical additives in food and beverages. Another very talented lady of this organization is Betty Lee Morales, who through her devotion to natural health has encouraged many women and men to give their professional attention to preventive medicine. The National Health Federation is perhaps more active than any organization in the United States in aiding the right of individuals to take the proper care of themselves without unnecessary governmental interferences. For example, with the help of Congressman James J. Delaney, Ninth Congressional District, New York, this organization assisted in preventing the government agencies from banning the sale of vitamins without a prescription.

"It's nice to be important, but it's more important to be nice" and "Love your fellow man for what he is and don't dislike him for what he is not" are two expressions of Max J. Ruderian, who, in 1958, founded the American

Physical Fitness Research Institute (APFRI). President of this organization is Howard C. Long, a dynamic leader, author and columnist for total wellness in natural health. This organization will put you on its mailing list if you write to APFRI, 824 Morgana Drive, Bel Air, California 90049. A paperback book published under the direction of this organization and entitled *Health's-A-Poppin* (Pyramid Books, New York) is considered one of the best and most comprehensive books available on physical fitness. Each chapter is written for the ordinary person by leading authorities and medical experts on how you can better practice preventive medicine. APFRI is continually distinguishing its performance of bringing to the general public ways and means of better living for a more natural world.

You Can Be Better than You Are

If you won't give your own energy a chance to help yourself and others, no techniques or advice will be of aid. For understanding there must be the desire to understand. An outstanding psychiatrist has said, "The most difficult thing for human beings is to face up to their mistakes and not let these imperfections depress further behavior." If you are a quitter you are missing the greatest experience of Life, working for a continued flow of energy in balance with you and God. In our book *The Magnetic Effect*, we stated that "animals, like man, live in an electromagnetic environment, continually bombarded with visible and invisible electromagnetic energies that affect behavior, health and welfare. . . . Man is a precise functioning biological system. This system functions with a balance of natural energies. An imbalance of the system is related to a physical or an emotional cause, or a combination of both. . . . If there is not proper care of the living system, then imbalances will continue to occur, regardless of the aid and assistance furnished to that system." If the human body is more natural in its upkeep, the natural powers of the body will function better in its release of natural energies. The energy of a healer is not just released from the healer, nor is it just modulated to the energy of the recipient. There is also the constant flowing in and out of these energies in the human system from the electromagnetic environment.

This is not a book that gives you techniques, as so many books do, that you cannot accomplish without many prerequisites. No, everyone has the natural energies for The Rainbow in Your Hands. Many of you will perform when your energies are not in balance. You will, however, perform more effectively by applying the understanding we have presented, and you will know you are with Nature and with God.

What Is Our Path?

Government agencies are spending millions of your dollars to show the need for more medical professionals. Why not more of this money to help the public know about preventive medicine? Don't we want to know more how to avoid illness and disease? All of you know nongovernmental organizations that function to fill this lack from your governmental bureaucracies. Take a good look at those who are crowding into medical facilities, taking space in waiting rooms, for stomach and headache pills, Band-Aid-like wrappings, other matters, that prevent the seriously ill from receiving quick and proper treatment. Think how much more time and assistance medical persons can give to those desperately in need if we all could learn and practice just a little more self-help to ourselves and others.

A leading medical authority of our acquaintance said to us, "There should be a law or strong requirements for medical graduates that all medical practitioners are educated to instruct their patients in preventive medicine. More emphasis is needed on preventing an occurrence than treating symptoms. No medical professional can cure anyone of anything. The final cure rests in each person. Medical procedures are only aids that prolong the time available for self-help. In the long run you cannot aid a person who will not aid himself."

There is a rising dangerous shortage in our societies of medical professionals. Hospitals and doctors' offices are overcrowded. Cost of medical services, including increased insurance rates for these costs and for malpractice expenses, are already out of reach for increasing numbers in our societies. Human stresses of our societies are forcing more young persons to take their lives. There is an alarming rate of young housewives, suffering from periods of depression, who respond with acts of violence against their own children and their husbands. Rising prices, shortages, increased unemployment and lack of job security, changing moral values, are increasing the number of emotionally disturbed in our societies. In our government, as in most governments of today, from the local to the national level, more laws and restrictions are making day-to-day existence impossible. There is no wonder that many of us find it difficult to face these stresses in our lives. Governments have become overworked, overburdened, and farther from the people. You are taxed on about everything from birth to death, including your birth and your funeral. Governments spend billions of dollars in promoting their attempted prestige with other nations while their peoples literally go begging in the streets.

Return to Nature

Peoples of the world are responding by turning to the Nature of things. They want to learn more how they can help themselves and not depend upon the authorities of governments. More attention by the peoples is being directed to the educational procedures. Violence is evident from the use of so-called modern textbooks in the schools, colleges and universities. Education instructs that humanity comes from a far-removed species of primate life forms. We have reached out in space to the infinite while we are educating that the beginning of man evolved from lower life. Therefore, it is said that man is himself the only intelligence and power of divinity, and there is nothing new that can be explained scientifically without this evolving concept.

These same modern teachings are offered to children in massive volumes of home reading by a number of large and well-advertised publishers. Our Western society seems content to condition the child's mind against the existence of God before formal education can attempt this conversion. This destructive mode of educational presentations is fast destroying many of our young people today. Without a moral sense of responsibility with a dedicated belief in God, there is no respect or purpose in the past, present or future. Children are being educated to be Godless creatures that become adults with no time nor concern for others nor their own bionic masterpiece of Nature.

Stresses of our societies exist with the children as well as adults. Consider the mind of the child torn between two factions. In the home and in religion the child is taught there is a living God. Then the child is forced into the modern world and society that allows no prayers in schools. To pass grades the child must learn what educators choose to instruct. They are taught that God did not create the Earth, in fact, man descended from a fish that crawled from the sea and evolved into a crawling, walking creature with no life after this life. How can we expect adults to have a healthy mind with a natural healthy outlook upon Life when we consider the morals of right and wrong so early conflicting the children in our age? So, why be decent at all? If there is no life beyond this life, why not any means to acquire material comforts against the freedom of others?

Laws made by man will never replace the knowledge that a power exists that is greater than man. The thinking man, woman—and child—knows there is a guiding power greater than ourselves, our own intelligence and comprehension, and more enduring than our societies. True belief in God cannot be swayed nor can the power of prayer be denied. The belief in God and in the power of prayer are the two greatest natural healing forces in existence. Some things are as they are, and no words, means, dogmas, inventions, will change their being. The bionic masterpiece of Nature is man, existing in, with, and among the natural energies of God, expressed in The Rainbow in Your Hands.

Give Nature a Chance

We hope in part this book will call to the attention of many mature men and women in the nations of the world today the need for their help and understanding of the young and older citizens, their stresses of societies, the need for compassion that has never been as great in the history of the world. We all see the distressed faces of the young and older persons in their despair and futility.

You Are Needed

You can give a smile, a warm greeting, a helping hand, to make your life and that of others worth living. A little effort on your part, the desire to act, with calm sincerity in your inner strength, and you will know what you must do. "A smile is your umbrella" by which you arm yourself with Faith, reflected from your face and in your positive manner, your thoughts, your helping hands, in The Rainbow in Your Hands.

Afterword

The techniques and understandings in this book apply to all persons in all societies, regardless of race, religion, faith and creed. Whatever your position in your culture you can use the information presented to help yourself and others.

What often seems wrong in Nature is actually man's misuse of Nature. Plants, vegetation, air, water, others of Nature's beauties, are not used correctly, and Nature responds to that misuse. Peace and Order to man can only be by progression in his comprehension of Nature.

In The Rainbow in Your Hands the proper energy use for the desired result is necessary, as in all Nature's ways. It is the sincere hope of your authors that this book will help your Life and the Life of others.

The Authors

About the Authors

ALBERT ROY DAVIS, scientist, was born in Halifax, Nova Scotia. As professor of physics, he taught physics, aerodynamics and electronics, establishing the Albert Roy Davis Research Laboratory at Green Cove Springs, Florida, in 1938. He has authored over 300 general science courses adopted for grade schools, high schools and colleges in the United States and many nations of the world. Recipient of a number of honorary doctors degrees for his scientific investigations, he is considered an accepted authority, and the founder, of the Science of Biomagnetics.

WALTER C. RAWLS, JR., scientist, lawyer, was born in Richmond, Virginia. His sociological and scientific investigations have taken him to many countries of the world as a consultant to governments and world organizations. He is acknowledged in national and international directories and is a member of the American Association for the Advancement of Science and the New York Academy of Sciences.

The Albert Roy Davis Research Laboratory can be reached via P.O. Box 655, Green Cove Springs, Florida 32043.